SOMEWHERE
IN A TOWN
YOU NEVER KNEW EXISTED
SOMEWHERE

For TARA,
I SO I GLAD
to RECONNECT.
ENJOY XO,
NINA

# SOMEWHERE
## IN A TOWN
## YOU NEVER KNEW EXISTED
## SOMEWHERE

NINA HART

*SUNDER PRESS · ASHEVILLE, NC*

SUNDER PRESS
Asheville, NC
828-254-3586
www.writingfromthetopofyourhead.com

Ordering information: Please contact the publisher for special discounts available on quantity purchases.

Editing by Lindig Harris
Cover photo © Josiane Keller
Cover and interior design by Douglas Gibson
Author photo © Sarah Whitmeyer

This is a work of fiction. Names, characters, places and incidents either are products of the author's imagination or are used fictitiously. Any resemblance to actual persons, living or dead, events or locales is entirely coincidental.

Excerpt from "Waking Early Sunday Morning" and "Where the Rainbow Ends" from COLLECTED POEMS by Robert Lowell. Copyright © 2003 by Harriet Lowell and Sheridan Lowell. Reprinted by permission of Farrar, Straus and Giroux, LLC.

Printed in the United States of America

Publisher's Cataloging-in-Publication Data

Hart, Nina (Nina B.)

    Somewhere in a town you never knew existed somewhere / Nina Hart. -- First edition, January 2015. -- Asheville : Sunder Press, [2015]

        pages ; cm.

        ISBN: 978-0-9905394-0-7
        Includes bibliographical references.
        Summary: The book speaks directly to society's "elephants in the living room" through kooky hooliganism and satire. The dreamlike stories skid apart and reunite, breaking time/space / reality rules, requiring the reader to have an imagination and be willing to stretch it beyond normal fictional boundaries.--Publisher.

    1. Prose poems, American. 2. Short stories, American. 3. Experimental poetry. 4. Literature, Experimental. 5. Surrealism (Literature) 6. Nature--Fiction. 7. Ecology--Fiction. 8. Educational tests and measurements--Political aspects--Humor. 9. Children--Fiction. 10. Loneliness--Fiction. 11. Magic realism (Literature) 12. Dystopias-- Fiction. 13. Speculative fiction. 14. Utopian fiction. I. Title.

PS3608.A7866 S66 2015                        2014946435
813/.6--dc23                                1410

*For the children, the elephants, and poet Robert Lowell.*

# CONTENTS

# A FINE DINNER OUT

There once was a writer who wrote because he had to. Not because he was exceptionally smart or funny. Not because of any high intelligence or worldliness. No one knew him to be a writer, because when they spoke to him he was quiet and did not appear to be very smart. He was not good at conversation. He didn't know the dates of wars or the names of French words. He didn't even know what "foie gras" was. If he tried to tell someone he was a writer they would offer him advice like "Well, if you're really a writer, then you need to write," not knowing that he was writing. He was writing all the time. "You need to write in order to be a writer," they would advise him.

The writer had grown up around intellectuals who had very sticky brains. Historical facts and trivia stuck to their brains like caramel, like fly paper, like jelly in a jar. He could view the facts through the clear glass but it was all just out of his reach.

One fine day, a young couple of ample means sat at an eatery table with him. Speaking about their real estate, their recipes for cranberry sponge bread and hand-made Indian curry. And then there were their trips to Italy to acquire the best balsamic vinegars. Talking all the time while chewing and still talking about their trips to Italy to acquire the best balsamic vinegars. And then the young woman said, "Will you join us for NPR's Collected Shorts at the theater? Where the readers read the writer's work?"

Instead of answering, the writer decided to think about how just this last week he had to present a poster to a group of people. Everyone else's posters were elaborately constructed. His was just a series of "blobs" that he'd spent a lot of time on. When he presented it he said "Don't you just like a blob sometimes? Don't you just like a blob?"

The writer glanced up from his forked meal as if witnessing the end of a short story. He had been treating himself to a dinner out because the half can of tuna and boiled (frozen) broccoli he had eaten in his apartment hadn't quite done it for him. In fact he was feeling quite faint as he walked into the dinner establishment. Lately he had been rationing protein for financial reasons. Only a half can of tuna. Only a half can of sardines or beans or only ten almonds or only two tablespoons of peanut butter. He stared at the young couple blankly, having no clever answers or retorts. He sat feeling guilty about paying twelve dollars for his meal of chicken and mashed potatoes with leeks. He sat wondering where his next meal money might come from. Then he imagined himself wolfing down the thirty dollar ticket to Collected Shorts with a nice fat béarnaise sauce. He desperately needed to feel that full feeling. Though now that the chicken and leeks and potatoes were entering his bloodstream, his dizziness was starting to subside. Still, the eatery and all of its inhabitants were continuing to whirl in quiet circles around him. Especially the faces of the young couple, blurring in and out of view as if he was sitting on a see-saw in the midst of a gentle wind. His face felt stretched long and his mouth numb and he felt a bit silly.

To the young couple he finally responded with "Don't you just like a blob sometimes? Don't you just like a blob?"

His own face felt like a wet blob as he spoke, his spongy mouth seemed turned inside out, the insides of his lips shone bumpy and red.

Uncomfortable, the young couple scratched their forks along the highways of their half-empty plates, drawing strange etchings with the tender blood of baby beets. Drawing circles in remnants of whipped goat cheese, saliva, and sauce étouffée.

"So long!" the writer says. And he goes home to feed his cat. He gives the cat a lot of extra food in case the cat has been hungry. He has no way to tell if the cat has been hungry because the cat can't talk and so he assumes the cat is hungry. The writer knows what it feels like to be hungry and so he makes sure the cat has more than enough food, even if the cat might get fat, because the cat, unlike himself, has no control over how much he will be fed, or when he will be fed, or if he will be fed. He lives at the mercy of the writer.

# CHIPPER DALE

Charles Chipper Dale stood dressed in the full regalia of an eight-year-old on his front lawn in Xenia, Ohio. The air was hot, and black, and sweet. Charlie jumped nervously from one foot to the other, nostrils flaring like a hunting dog's. "The tornado will hit without warning!" prophesized Chipper to his audience of six children, one dirty sparrow, and a beat-up red Tonka Truck. "We will all be dead, taken up into the wormlike mass, cold faces pressed against one another in the brutal raging wind!" The children all sighed and began to shake and cry. "I have to go home and get my Snoopy Roo-Roo." cried Ellen, who looked like a ringing bell in her oversized green dress. "Well the clouds will suck you up like a milkshake into the sky if you do, Ellen! I forbid you to go anywhere, Ellen." said Charlie. "Where are the parents? Where are the parents?" asked Jake Lacky, who had a wide chest just like his pot-smoking dad. "My teacher said I'm a latchkey kid. What's a latchkey kid?" No one knew. In the distance the raw smell of rain drew closer. The children could taste the mist as it slipped on their lips like hard candy. They could feel a rumble in the earth under their hot tennis shoes. "What do we do, Charlie?" asked Rainbow, one of Jake Lacky's three siblings, latchkey kid and daughter of the pot smoker. "Look to the wind." said Charles Chipper Dale, fingers twitching, eyes veering off into the far distance. "It's here, it's coming, and it won't be long. We won't wait for the sirens to go off. We're children. We can *feel* things. Let's head on down to the root cellar, one at a time. Single file." "I love you all so much," whispered Rainbow, as she held her brother Jake's hand and followed him down the stone staircase. Cars

4

and their drivers drove past the children on the street. Faces and heads and necks propelled forward on their way back to work after lunch break. All of them ignoring the twisting sky in the distance and the staunch smell of darkness. The tornado would hit without warning. The latchkey kids would be safe in Charlie Dale's root cellar, listening to the roaring sounds of the King of Winds. All of them holding hands and Rainbow mouthing I love you I love you and I love you all into the dark green landscape.

# BONANZA KEEP DIGGING

Bonanza was a scary girl, all backwards in her thinking. Five years old and she didn't like anyone. No-one liked her either. She often wondered which came first, did she like no-one and then did no-one like her, or was it the other way around?

"Shut up and keep digging," cried her mother, while Bonanza was busy burying the bony remains of her ten last, best and only friends. "Shut up and keep digging," mouthed Bonanza in a sour, mocking voice, hoping her mother didn't hear but secretly wishing she would. Bonanza was digging and stacking, digging and stacking, and burying her little toy dolls, one on top of another, digging and stacking and burying them all in the backyard.

"There goes Frances," she said, one by one patting them on the soft tops of their heads. "Little Limp Suzette, Astrid, Lingafore, Penitence, Rye Bread, Amber Ocean with the Amazing Marble Brown Eyes, Lori Fred the Beast, Marmalade." And then there was The Ancient One, who kept bobbing her loose plastic head back and forth, stacked flat on her back on top of Marmalade, in the ruddy brown dirt. "Stay still," said Bonanza through stinging tears.

These were the days of no return. Her mother was right. If she couldn't be a friendly, polite girl, then she would be liked by no-one. And so it was that her mother, with resounding voice, descended heavily down the porch stairs, thick ankled, to the backyard to supervise Bonanza's burial of the word f-r-i-e-n-d-s-h-i-p.

All the summer light grew dim, darker, until Bonanza was just a small speck of dust beating away at the backyard air, then, her self, buried. Fell in with the rest of them. Fell right flat on top of The Ancient One.

# JEANINE TELEVISED

The TV was tuned to channel five. The sound was on loud. On the screen was the face of an unruly young man, his mouth opening and closing like a poisonous puffer fish. Endless. Ceaseless. Jeanine, in her hotel room, stared at the box, flung her beer bottle straight at the screen and broke it through. Broke it through to the tubes and the wires. The insides saying boing boing. Buzz buzz.

Jeanine hated more than anything when people spoke too fast and too loud like this young man and what made it worse was he was trying to sell something. Pontiacs in fact. He sounded like all the children were sounding to her; speaking at the speed of lunatic video games, microchips, and algorithms. She couldn't keep up with their words, couldn't comprehend their rapid-fire sounds. Could no longer understand human language.

Jeanine felt like an old pinball machine on tilt. Her head was set on her neck slightly askew and with a dizzy wobble to her half-heeled walk. "Another motel room and another bottle through the moon." Beer and smoke and dark green carpet and bleached white towels rough on her empty face. And plastic water glasses wrapped in plastic and empty closets with those locked up hangers and signs that say Privacy Please. An unknown sky in an unknown town and rain pouring down the streaked windowpanes.

She scrawls a note to Lucia, the maid, on a comment card that says "How was your stay at Deer Valley Plaza?" It reads:

Please, if you find me, don't send me home. Really I am a real person filled with wonder and awe, only the thing, I mean probably what happened to me is that everyone        I

mean everyone      on earth        began to talk *too fast.*
*Too too      fast.      Too fast.*
     The          the          air conditioner          has
swallowed my whole body.                    Even my head
head                of hair. Yes          yes          I am in
there                and I am                          sorry
but I won't be able to          leave you      leave you
a tip.     A tip.
     With all of my love,
     Jeanine.

# NOTES FOR BOOK

1. Not sure where they live. Logan's Lake?
2. **Did the writer write the book?**
2. Elephants. Elephants. Elephants.
3. Jeanine asks for suggestions for *Movies You Would Like to See Made.*
4. Are the Pod People here?
5. Townspeople give Oratory Speeches in school auditoriums, or from the insides of air conditioners.
6. Poet Robert Lowell.
7. The sky is falling
8. Cow

# JEANINE'S ORATORY SPEECH FROM INSIDE THE AIR CONDITIONER (NO ONE IS IN THE ROOM TO HEAR IT)

You say, you say, But God, why am I here? But really, why am I here? You hear about saintly schoolteachers. You hear about nuns dressed in striped dish towels and Mother Teresa and nurses and polo players well who well who said that? Not a polo player for God's sake! Mama, when I grow up I wanna be a polo player! That's what I said, I tell them. Just what they say, just like that. I'll follow those polo players around, offer them a job at least. Polo players are finally paid money so at least they have a job. Not fair, you say, Well the world isn't fair. And there are entire families who think they are the best family in the world and they might be right. And then there are just the artists, the introverts, people off the scale of fashion. Joe, down the street, works as an attendant at a nursing home. No not an ad man, silly! An attendant. Says he likes it there. Takes the bus. And Rae, his girlfriend, may have scars, he may have beat her up but we know and the whole street knows we can hear him yelling. And I want to pick him up at the bus stop and take him somewhere but it's none of my business. I want to pick her up too and take her somewhere else but that's none of my business too. Or is it? Or is all fair in love and war and don't talk about it anyways. I still can't even talk to my own family. And I think I've gone so far. No I don't. I don't, don't even have the faintest idea how to talk to them. Or you! Some people you don't want to tick off anyways. They'll yell at you and then you'll have to drive them somewhere, anywhere, and leave them off. And then where will you be? If you leave off everyone in the whole world. Dump them off somewhere in the middle of the desert? Where will you be? Where will you be?

# EVERYTHING IS RETURNING

One stormy Saturday afternoon over at Logan's Lake, there stood one bulked-up, square-shaped cow. No-one knew how it got there. Still, it looked quite at home gazing off toward the fields and chewing rough pieces of broken grass. A small bit of spittle had gathered to the side of its lower lip. It appeared that the cow had something to say, some message for the people. The townspeople had gathered around to discuss this, but they couldn't figure out how to talk to a cow.

Witness to this matter was one Jason Fornborn. He was light on his feet and wore baggy pants on bone-eyed hips. The townspeople found Jason to be strange. Even though he had always lived in Longham, he never seemed to quite fit in. Strangely, he ate his breakfast for lunch and his lunch for dinner and sometimes dinner for breakfast. He was always confusing the waitresses at the local restaurants for this reason.

As Jason slouched closer to the crowd, the cow turned its head to look right at him. Jason was the first person the cow had looked at right in the eyes. Logan's Lake began to stir, blowing the little tips of its waves back as if it knew something interesting was about to happen.

Jason and the cow stood face to face, lip to lip, and at the same moment each split a grin. It was a moment of vast recognition. "Well my oh my," said Jason, "If this isn't my mother come back to see me!" The townspeople gasped and one even threw his fork at him. "Well well well, Jason," cried Mr. Lon Anderson, as he stepped widely forward. Mr. Lon Anderson was a respected former mayor of Longham. "Well, Jason, what makes you think this cow here is your mother?"

Jason replied "Oh, I can just tell, Sir. I recognize her!" Mr. Anderson observed "Well, she happens to be a bull. She's a male cow there, son! And your mother was a woman!" Jason reached down to pick up a blade of grass, stuck it between his teeth and crunched down. "Well yes, Mr. Lon Anderson, but you don't understand. Why, I used to be a little calf and this bull used to be my mother!" The townspeople gasped and swayed en masse. Thunder rattled in the distance, shaking Logan's Lake and all of its waves and borders. With a voice that resounded with great authority, Jason said "Now everything is returning to its rightful place."

# OOOF!

It was a quick thing that happened quickly. I didn't know where I was, or where I was going. Suddenly thrown down to the ground from our Flying Saucer Sauce vehicle. Dropped straight down. Ooof. Ooooof! Hoofed feet, no more rasping claws but more solid things white and heavy made of clear marble? I am heavy. Dry heaving in fact. Am I on dry land? Why I feel like a large... They're spying on me now. Staring. All I want to do is eat in peace. Nice long leaves of grass. Nice graceful long green stalks grind slowly in my mouth. Nice long views of fields and countryside. Wow, nice chompers I've got! They work well. Big thick jaws with slow moving spittle digest then spit up a little green belch. Why I think I see one or two more of me over in the distant field. Are we just all from everywhere? Is there no difference? Ah, Languria Languria our star home. I love my memories of Languria. Ah this thing called soil it seems the closest thing to Languria. Kick my hoof and it is dust. Slow head. Arching neck. I am bound to me. In this heavy plod I am gravity. And to think I had become accustomed to cafeterias. To standing and wait-ing in line with my tray. I am alone in this field oh over to my left I see a large water body. Drink drink boats and bobbers flash of light and surge. Whose mother am I? Ah yes I know this to be true. Can a cow smile? How does a cow smile? Do I draw my lips back like this?

The townspeople appear, standing in a circle around me. Patting me on my  head and neck. Bribing me with cubes of salt to please tell them anything. Anything.

Finally I open my mouth so they can see my wide gummy gums and I say:

It   is   we   cattle   who   are   not   cattle   but
genetically                 fondled                 cattle and we are,
well,          we are      fondled like your ears      of corn
are fondled      and we are      wondering                 if you
could be so kind                                         please
                          the exact recipe for the new test
tube                 saucy hamburger?
    In exchange for the saucy recipe we will give you      give
you      the recipe      for people gumbo      with brownish
cornstarch sauce          and          and      with    those
succulent ancient legs      and baby corn          and and then
promise          we will all stop landing      stop landing
on your          mustard and      sweet relish          hot dog
picnics.          Honestly.      We cows do solemnly swear on
a stack of Holy Wrangler Fitness Club Barbells

# SUZY AND HER FRIENDS
## WHO AREN'T SUZY

Logan's Lake is having a very special day today. The water is standing still and proud, barely a wave in sight. The smell of sewage and decayed fish lightly perfumes the air. A few pretty cows are loping gracefully along the circular paths. Meanwhile camera crews are setting up for the filming of a new reality TV show called "Unreality Suzy." One of the cows steps straight down on a sound cable and stalls in front of the humongous camera lens. Her round face stares in with curiosity. Her mouth chews in half circles.

In today's episode Suzy's friends have matched her up with a prospective mate named Tim. He has sent her a floating gift in a box that lays on top of a tiny raft, which is painstakingly crossing Logan's Lake to get to her. She waits interminably on the opposite shore, her long red hair fluting in the wind. I have to take a pee, she says to herself. She had only just met this man for the first time the day before and she feels scared and unsure of her connection to him. He happens to be rather large and this bothers her. Cameras are filming the little raft and zooming in and out and a commentator is describing the length of the waves and the velocity of the unpredictable trajectory. He finally says Look! I believe there's a diamond in the box! Could it be a ring? The gathering crowd gasps at the possibility of a proposal and the stray cow, who had been heaved back onto the path, lets out a huge methane fart. When the raft finally arrives on the shore Suzy runs to open the box and it turns out that the diamond is not a diamond; it is actually an abalone shell and not an engagement ring. Which makes a little bit of sense because the two of them haven't even known each other very long. And the commentator says You've got to admit, that abalone shell is beautiful.

Later, with the camera crews gone, Suzy walks along the lakeside. Circumambulating in great circles, box in hand. She had found a secret box inside of the first box. In the box she finds some tremendous sloping canyons that are almost falling apart. She finds some rattling boxcars on railroad trains and the red hairs of a fox and a tiny train conductor who is trying to talk to her but she can't understand a word he is saying and he gets so out of breath he just finally falls down exhausted. Poor old guy. And then she meets a tiny lady that lets her stay for 2 nights in a rental cabin for free. After she has rested, Suzy walks to the water's edge and falls deep into the lake. Another 2 days pass and she finally washes up onto the shore. The townspeople find her lying on her stomach on the wet pungent clay. The back of her neck looks like someone else's so she can't recognize herself and neither can anyone else.

It turns out she just needed a little time alone to think about her life. Right?

All of a sudden the sky turns pink and a big white heart with veins appears in the sky, with huge swollen blood vessels reaching down to the ground.

Lightning starts crashing and hitting people and we all scatter. I run toward the acupuncture school, but I can't get in the front door because the building is made of pure solid metal! Bam I hit my head and fall to the cement! Bam! Lots of trees are falling around me and I almost get hit by a tree!

I decide to go and talk to the marshmallow chocolate bunnies at my brother's house. Apparently, one of the bunnies has a hurt shoulder so I am going to do some Reiki on it.

It's good to have a mission.

## AND NOW INTRODUCING
## POET ROBERT LOWELL
## WHO WENT TO HARVARD

Hello my name is dead Poet Robert Lowell and I am reapplying to college. I know you have not seen me in about 30 years. I am sorry. I needed to be quiet. I have been following around street people, filmmakers, sex addicts, performance artists, and waitresses. Sure I know Bedford, Medford, and sure I know Barry Escapade. Please would you sneak me back into college? Or high school would be just fine.

My brother Lint is here with me, too.

## LUCIA VISITS JEANINE DAILY

Lucia pulls up a chair in front of the air conditioner. She lowers her head and scrunches her eyes to see if she can see Jeanine. Jeanine, she whispers, Jeanine. I brought you pancakes. Jeanine lets out a short whelp and her thumb and index finger slide out from between the metal grates. Strawberry? Jeanine's mouth waters. Yes, strawberry. Butter melts and syrup pours down over the top of the cakes and each piece is cut into precise half-inch squares. Fed one by one, slowly, through the cold rainy grates.

# SOMEWHERE IN A TOWN YOU NEVER KNEW
# EXISTED SOMEWHERE

Of course we've all heard the saying All the world's a stage. But it really is a stage - a shadowy proscenium. Just go walking. Say 8 o'clock on a winter's night. Just go trudging in your big green boots through your neighborhood. See all the houses lit up like a stage set. Wrinkled curtains sit stodgily against a creamy background. A large female figure slowly lifts a suitcase inside the sadly lit room. Across the street you can see baby blue lights shining out through opaque windows. And then the next house looks like Boo Radley's with its gothic fences and all. The requisite howling of cats, and a dog named Molly, and the oddly human murmur of cars in the distance. A '68 Dodge truck suddenly comes up from behind, real close, and you move to the grassy edge of the road, huddle close out of the way of the thick high-beams. Your grey woolen hat becomes lit up in this heavily snowed air. Particles of light whirl around you. Caught like a famous moment in the spotlight. Your hat feels almost warm on your head. You feel regal, like the Queen of England, while the lights of the truck go spinning away. You trudge in your green boots back to your own house and the curtains come down. Your personal show has ended. Your sleep arrives, eyelids shut.

# BIG MAN BILL

He was a gentle giant, big-shelled and barrel-chested like a clam, with a mouth that stretched from hemisphere to hemisphere, veins that shone through from under the skin of his face, looking like a light blue map of Vermont. Highways of blood up front and coursing down his thin notebook page of skin, steering wildly around the corners of his face, making loops around his ears, hoops around his lips. Torn crackly paper spots around the tenderness of his eyes. Clam-backed and ridge-shelled. Puffed up and hard on the outside, tender on the inside. He strove daily not to fall out of himself. For who would be there to pick him up? Baggy blue jeans held him in and bump-bump-bump on the seat of his '68 dodge truck, hands all daring at the wheel, curving round the turns and turning round the curves. He was nobody's husband, heading home for dinner, white plastic bag full of fresh smiling shrimp in the seat next to him. At home he'd cook them with butter and garlic, he'd feed some to the cat, he'd be all quiet with the night, quiet with the cat on the front porch, quiet with the sky, looking out at the broad range. He turned 65 today, and it was his last day of work. Packed up the navy blue hardback books, wiped down the dust from the tops of drawers, caressed the wheels of his file cart one last time. Yes, today the big man turned 65. Sitting on the porch with his cat.

# DEE DEE IBERSTALL

She wore her pink nightgown with ferocity, teeth bared. All day and all night. Never changed out of it. Changed her shoes sometimes. She'd sip dry pink drinks in it. Thin black straw slides to the left as her lips careen to the right. All the neighbors were scared of her as they watched her pace behind plate glass windows, panting. Rumor was, she'd killed her husband. He used to sit rocking in the wicker chair on the front porch, TV on, round red hands on the remote, staring and laughing at the talking box, mouthing words and pointing at worldwide images. Occasionally, he'd turn his neck, crook'd like a baby snake, spotting a neighbor walking a poodle, wave a quick hello—shorter than a breath. In the morning he was a coffee drinker on his dew-fogged porch. Steaming red tongue and red lips and sometimes winter air. Even with the coffee he would fall asleep maybe 15 minutes later, his rocking chair creaking on the musty wooden floor. You would never see them speak to one another. She was the tiger and he the house cat. They would pass each other without a word. Vaporous ghosts living in separate glass mazes. Then one day he disappeared. The neighbors would say "Where is Bill? Where is Bill? Why he hardly ever leaves his porch." Indeed, he hardly ever left his neighborhood proscenium, 396 Oliver St, where lampshades froze as shy silhouettes, sheer curtains revealed cold pink nightgowns, revealed disappearances, like in Argentina, Mexico, places on the news, places that disappear behind false existences, straws for drinking up tight lips and muffled gurgling secrets. Her laugh is a cackle. He appears falsely as a snake. Slithering into a night of brown stripes and shadows.

# LIPTON

I might imagine I am mad. I might suspect I am mad. Yes I really might be mad. Yes, I really am mad. It's not about the pancakes, or the soup, or the milk you spilled, or the pair of underwear. It's not about the melted Milky Way, the day you took a pickax to the freezer, the day you wrote on the bathroom wall fuck you in tiny letters, thinking I wouldn't notice. It's more about the little things. The little things.

It's like I only exist in a tinny soup can! You see me. I know you see me. I flit by out of the corner of your eye. I am asking you how your day was. Are you hungry? Do you want some soup? But all you do is grunt like a bovine! Like a punching bag of popcorn! I wasn't the one who set you on fire that day! You were the one who dropped your cigarette when you fell asleep watching Madame K on the Hot Box! You weren't the furious one! That night Oh No! Oh I could spittle! Oh I could spit with such fury! No more Pop Tarts they make you crazy! And then you complain about the way I wiggle what kind of ham are you? My head is a garage door and it's finally opening! My eyes are lampshades that snap and roll, snap and roll. How can I fix your breakfast when all I can do is kick kick kick the bag of Fritos! The toast is burning! See? My ears are pointy and devil red! You can touch them they feel hot. I smell like a white dove, anchovy, caution, Lipton Soup remember Lipton Chicken Noodle Soup? Soup? Want some? Something of a comfort there. So now do I have your attention? I wish you'd stop dragging that chair across the floor. Right and left and right and left and left and right.

# IS THAT YOU, DOBSON?

How do you weigh the life of a fish? It's not ordinary to possess a big Italian mob face, an under-bite, poppy eyes and boo-boo lips. These are the fish of the Woods Hole Oceanic Research Center. Tanks are open to the public. Fish tanks containing all number of wild faces darting about. Al Pacino, Barbara Streisand, Bob Hope. Fish movie stars with cigars. Amputees. A fin missing. Sloughed scales float up to the rim of the tanks. Icicle seaweed. Manta Ray.

The picture is bleak. Dobson, who works at the research center, swings a sloshing bucket in his right hand filled with an assortment of worm creatures. Dobson swings and walks, swings and walks, and the tourists absently watch as he pushes and grunts past them, edgily, as if he's carrying his own heavy squirming secret.

Dobson pulls a scale out of his pocket, wheezes, and plants the bucket firmly, begins to weigh handfuls of muddy worms. "Last mud you're gonna see," he mumbles. He portions them into plastic cups on a wet green table, feels the ranting squirming alive around his dirty nailbeds. Doesn't know what to do about this ranting. Thinks about the wife left behind and the day the townspeople crowded around after he'd fainted like a pale white dove. Washed up flat on his back in the street. It was the day he couldn't find the watering can. The day his memory played tricks on him. The day he realized that if he didn't leave town right that very moment then he would suffocate, or worse, dry up like a fish out of water. Or he might have to tell the real story of what happened to him. The real story behind

Longham. He wasn't ready to do that. Besides, he'd always liked fish, their awful smell, metallic scales, and naked flat eyes that would glow, even in the hottest of waters.

# BUTTERFLY FARM

It had been years since she'd been to the butterfly farm. She had to stop going because the butterflies were too beautiful. She would sit and weep as their soft wings skimmed overhead and grazed her tiny ears. Their grand wings veering wide in flight and showing her prints like African batik.

She didn't like being the one who always cried, sitting on the bench and looking down and over to the side. She was trying to hide the tears that rolled out like curling butterfly tongues. The butterflies didn't know she was crying for them. They were too busy landing on velvety flowers and sucking sweet liquids out of squeaky golden stems.

The last day she spent at the butterfly farm was the day she cried the most. She was sitting on a bench and she was talking to them. She told them they were "sweet and gentle" in a very loud voice, which surprised even her. Suddenly a slow-moving man wearing dirty beige cover-alls and holding a heavy glass jar began to walk toward her. He came and took her four favorite butterflies. She didn't know how he knew. He stuffed them with his rough hands through the top of the jar and quickly screwed on the lid, their tiny wings wilting. Dogs barked and birds screeched and the sky turned grey with sadness. Some big bowl of hunger grew up in her and puffed her size up to the clouds. Swollen hands moving like giant wings. Her love was that big. She took the man's bulbous arm and threw it behind his back and arrested him and took him back to the pork farm and the butterflies now sit on his shoulder and eat from dog bowls for all the rest of their days.

# STICKY LITTLE FEET

The wicked witch knew she had a large wet wart on her chin. She found it pretty, that is, when she wasn't trying to hack it off with a saw! She found her twisted feet stylish, that is, when she wasn't busy dropping houses on them! She found her hunched back gorgeous, except when she'd beat it with the stick of a broom! Sometimes she would have her flying monkeys beat on her back while she was in mid-air, just for fun!

The witch tells herself the story that she was born out of an egg and hatched in a pumpkin patch on October 31st 1919. It was a good year. The moon rose over the corn and she rose fully formed, on her broom, the full moon behind her.

The witch had sticky little feet when she took her shoes off, so she never ever took them off lest she get stuck. She had greasy hair never washed, and green skin that cracked and peeled like a molting snake, especially if she cackled or crowed too hard. She carried a purse like the other ladies would, but she laughed because it had nothing in it, well sometimes a stolen sparrow's egg. Oh how pure and how lonely she was, just she and the full moon. Gasping at their beauty.

When the witch was young she was befriended by two boys who called her their sister. They beat her up and threw her down and beat her up and threw her down. She would laugh as they shook her and pretend not to notice. She pretended it didn't hurt, though it did, it really did. They did all kinds of bad things to her and then they threw her out at night into the field of shadows, where crisp apples swooned and cats growled and mated. Where worms squirmed and kicked up the earth under her feet and branches of slowly growing trees quickened at the sight of her, twisting long and looming large, trying to strangle her in the moonlight so she could get no sleep. Sometimes a man who called himself her father would come by in a tractor and mow her over. She was too ugly, he thought, and would be better made into topsoil for his farm of onions, and recycled. Where did she come from anyways? One day I called her daughter but I don't know why. Why, I must have been drunk! He'd plow her under and she would tunnel her way out with dirt in her mouth and wait in the piles of manure until she could escape in the morning. She'd escape, and a black cloud would follow her all day. Stinking and floating and bloating like a mule.

## A MOVIE BONANZA WOULD LIKE TO SEE:

Hello Bonanza this is your Mother I'm writing to you on a brand-new computer that Dad bought for me and it is unbelievable and I'm talking to you and on the screen it's writing what I'm saying like magic. Anyhow we gently got back from dinner and your Father had a cake waiting for us and we had cake and ice cream but before that we had a wonderful Italian dinner. Dad and I had Eggplant Parmesan and Daisy had Chicken Cacciatore and we had a terrific salad and spaghetti.
   Love
   Mom

# A MOVIE THE WITCH WOULD
# LIKE TO SEE MADE

A close-up of a lumberjack's ear as he's wielding his chain-saw up and over his head and down and back through the soft and hard dust of an old-growth redwood tree. Around his ear you can see the swinging, and flying pieces of bark, and the white light of sawdust filtering through the herds of standing trees. Redwoods weep and wail and down the ridge you can hear crying choruses of ponderosa pines.

A man and a woman are talking. The sound is turned off and somehow there is a pressure in your own ears as you watch. The pressure grows stronger and stronger and stronger. Enter from left an old yellow Labrador Retriever barking without a voice box.

A row of twelve Valencia oranges are rolling in perfect precision down a hill in Dharamsala, India. Six monkeys are following in close pursuit. This film is done in very slow motion.

Her mother is 5 years old, glaring into the lens of an old Brownie camera. The camera follows, snapping blurry photos as her brothers chase her down dry hallways. The walls pitch to the right and the ceilings sag down with weight. Her grandmother's face is partially hidden. There is no one there to save her mother as her brothers lie on top of her and do things to her that they shouldn't know how to do. Albert Einstein appears, trying to explain the exact nature of the neurotic Jewish family, its violent history, the music that still, despite it all, comes out of it like rows of ancient violins singing in the red-lit darkness.

# KILLER

Okay. I'll say it. I'm a killer. I kill, maim, destroy, murder. It's me and I'm it, her, him, he, she. I tear you down, break you apart, naked, you squirm your last squirms and I throw you away.

You, you're small, innocent, and wild. I take you from your mates, families, and tribes. I take oxygen from your water and pour sludge down your throats. I have no feelings about this. I don't want to go to your pain. I am your killer and so is the guy next to me. The guy making coffee. The guy selling maps and the science major. The drum majorette. We're all your killers.

I tell myself stories and fairy tales. I tell myself you must have volunteered to be drowned in a sea of oil, which you inhale through your smooth and perfectly arranged gills. "I love you" I say, as I kill you. No wonder you swim away at the sight of us.

I make up stories. That you volunteered for this. To slowly starve to death as we take your food, your plankton. I open a small flat object with a screen and letters and I talk to myself like I'm somebody. Talk about exams and where I'll get coffee and you're starving pleading and running and somewhere I'm remembering that I am smelling you. Your soup your sea your salt your land of hope. I can scoop your destiny in my hand like sand. I watch it run through my fingers. I remember your eyes and nose and mouth and you are waiting and pleading and I am empty.

I tell myself stories that you volunteered to sacrifice your bodies in a sea of oil so that certain ones of us could awaken. I tell myself you were smart enough to want to die as a martyr, millions of you floating in a sea of black blood. Your lips and tongues taste suffocation your shoulders sinking your sleek power you surrender even it. Sucking surrendering feathers fall from the sky. Even the birds in the air sink like stones somewhere over there, we say, somewhere else, somewhere over there. A froth of blood gasping. You volunteered for this so sleeping sloth slow killers could stop killing in slow motion.

I tell myself stories at night, bed-time stories. Secretly big brown bears and roly-poly raccoons dress in pink chiffon and have parties where they serve peanut butter cookies and green beans and soft jelly donuts. Strawberry shortcake. They dance together bear and raccoon. They dance to sliding hillsides and tornados. Honey jar falls off the table and breaks.

Just because we can't see that far into the deep we forget. Think octopus, bluefin tuna, burrowing crab, sea turtle with the checkerboard belly.

I tell myself stories so I don't have to say thank you. For your schools of glowing neon, slippery flat faces, rough sandpaper skin, blow-hole last of the human race what are we I ask. What are we?

Worst of all, I tell myself the story that you cannot feel love. Worst of all I tell myself the story that I cannot feel love.

## PARADE DREAM

We're pushing a gigantic stuffed elephant with real ivory tusks through our town. The elephant is on a rickety wooden platform with wheels. They let us join the parade but then we wreck the parade with our heavy sorrow and faces wet with tears.

# IS THERE ENOUGH BLOOD?

"This is an exercise," the doctor of research said. He was a well-respected doctor. Or you could say he was a doctor feared by all. The doctor said to his subjects If I find even one of you hiding and not wanting to come out for this experiment, I'm going to drag you down to the stockroom and tie you down! I'm going to put your feet in your slippers and plug in your earplugs. You won't mind the icy syringe, but, but, I seem to be turning quickly from doctor to, to, small mice, I mean small mouse that is. This is tricky now, I mean I'm drooling, my face is grey with, with, fur, biting chomping I feel so light, lithe, all of me compact, my slight bones, delicate, my organs pressed up to my little ribs, why, I smell like a barnyard! Hey, can somebody help me? I don't like how this exercise is turning out! It was supposed to be just a test! At least I am not Bob the Goat. Huh? OK stop laughing at me! I don't know if any of you know Doctor Sludgy? Well, call him! Call my friends! Sludgy! Is there enough blood? Can you hook my paw back up to the drip? The tubes, it's in the tubes, try the x factor. The one made from the Icelandic ash. I'm sorry I bossed you all around so much, took you for granted. I'm going down down no no where's the hole? It's not working underground railroad nonstop to New York City. Sewer rat section first class ticket please. That'll be fine. Window seat. I like to smell the ocean. Who's president? I've been through wilder times in the 60's. Waiter could I please order a sweet? Have we capsized? My paws are slipping. My little claws are clasping and skidding. Opening and closing. Making claw marks and leaving nail clippings in the wood.

# NOBODY LIVES HERE ANYMORE

They don't live here anymore. The Colberts don't live here anymore. That's what the Rawlings family said to the movers who pulled up in their blue truck with a painting of the whole world on it. They don't live here anymore. You can go in and see for yourselves. Doors open and nothing inside. I think maybe we saw their cat skulking around. Couldn't catch it.

The movers looked at each other and tilted their heads as if trying to understand slurred words. Jesse, the smaller of the movers, said to Angus, the larger of the movers Well I wonder when they moved out they just called us last night. Scheduled a move and all. The Rawlings family looked a bit strained and strange and were reluctant to answer questions. Besides, they said it was Sunday and they had just been to church and the pastor had talked about "happy endings." The Rawlings family shook their heads up and down and said they loved a happy ending. They nodded and said they were All about happy endings. Bill Rawlings pulled a toothpick out of his baggy pants pocket. He had been keeping it there for times of emergency. He began to suck on the toothpick, pull it through his incisors, poke it at his gums until he could taste the salt of his own blood. He began to poke a spot harder and harder so when he opened his mouth and smiled at Jesse and Angus, a tinge of red had coated his teeth. So subtle that they hardly noticed themselves feeling even a bit more uncomfortable as they stood in front of the barren house. They wondered what to tell their boss when they came back empty handed. Meanwhile Bill Rawlings put his arm around his young son Andy. Andy had strawberry red hair. He had tiny shoulders that had lodged in a vice grip around his neck. Andy's eyes were studying the ground, the bits and pieces of leaves and twigs. His eyes left the ground and swept their way around to the empty house and its sullen windows. Bill invited Jesse and Angus inside to have a look-see. Mrs. Rawlings offered them a slice of pound cake on a paper napkin. Mrs. Rawlings offering them a smooth smile through peach lipstick. Jesse looked at Angus and back at the Rawlings family. Saying politely well I'm sorry but I think Angus and I better get back to the office. They had scheduled other moves for the day. They had to get lunch. They had to find a lost book they had lost. They said they had run out of a special blue bungee cord and had to go buy some more. They pulled out of the driveway. Jesse and Angus pulled their sputtering truck with the whole world painted on it back down the street and out of this neighborhood.

# TWILIGHT OF THE GODS

It is the Twilight of the Gods, and there is still no rain. I am shaking and clutching my blue umbrella in the bright sun on the corner of 5ᵗʰ Avenue and Broadway, near the famous Shake Shack. Behind me is the sliding metal door of the Persian grocery. With a startle and a slap, the grand curtain comes up. I twirl around and there is my good friend Fasul, grinning ear to ear with stained teeth and toothpick, coming at me with hand out-stretched. "Hello Scary Monster!" He says, with Persian accent. "How is Scary Monster today?" I hunch forward, his words hit me like a basket of hail. I can't help it if they hurt even though I like him. I grip my blue umbrella closer so I can cover the softest part of the back of my neck. I hiss through my teeth and say "Scary Monster is fine today. Please don't hurt Scary Monster. Scary Monster waits for rain. Scary doesn't want pomegranate today." Just then Fasul shoots out his daily dish of hot purple pink seeds and slants it in the direction of Scary. Fasul laughs, "No seeds today, Scary?" "No, no seeds for Scary today," Scary looks the other way and begins to bob his knees up and down. From down the long street a passerby walks toward Scary in a pin-striped suit. He tilts his body away from Scary's body as if Scary has bad smells. "Why is everyone going away from Scary?" Scary asks Fasul. Scary's body begins to sweat and shake more violently, as if he's trying to shake a virus out of his skin, as if he's crying through his pores and all his insides are spilling out into the curbs and corners of New York City streets. Plastic bottles begin to float by in Scary's sweat and flies feast on Scary's tears. Scary is so wet now and he is glad the sun is there to dry him out. "Now Scary loves the sun."

Scary tells Fasul. Fasul's brown-stained teeth break open wide into a smile. Later, as night grows near and Scary's umbrella casts a dark shadow across his bearded face, even Scary knows that now is still the Twilight of the Gods.

# STRESS TEST

Say anything, said Dr. Spungen, as he sticks his penlight straight at the man's eye. I, I don't know what to say, Dr. Spungen. I don't know who you are. I don't know why I'm here or what you're doing. You're trying to poke a hole in my eyelid! No, said Dr. Spungen. We test all veterans. Just home from the war are you? Well yes of course yes, the man said. His name is Raincoat. Full name Full Scary Raincoat, like Full Metal Jacket. Raincoat with one eye open and only nine fingers. Count them. Raincoat with knife in pocket. Scary Raincoat gripping a half-ripped photograph of his family. Half of son Jimmy. Half of daughter April. Half of wife Winnie. Raincoat sputters and looks with his one good eye at Spungen. Said I didn't think this was a cooking class! I can count my fingers for myself, thank you! Spungen takes a long deep breath. Raincoat continues. What is this, a stress test? A memorial service at my empty grave? I'm not dead yet, just half alive. I can't tell you which half. Can you figure out that much? So what, are you going to send me home with a box of licorice? Well what I got won't take stringy black licorice! I'm spinning around and around. I can't hold on anymore. Where I've been you'll never know but I pay for your job how dumb is that? Spungen sighs and reluctantly takes out his vise grip. Places it on the side of Raincoat's arm and pinches his pink hairless skin. So this is the quickest, easiest way Raincoat. To forget what it is you don't want to remember. Scary's one good eye glances down to the floor below, the red floor below. Shadows of Koi fish float like death shadows, barely setting sun, rustling sounds of flowers and lonely aching for home. And the desire to feel nothing, nothing touching his skin any more. Ever again.

# THE HISTORIC LAVENDER WARS

I am the official lavender flower holder for my army battalion. There are big strapping men in my unit but it is my job to go first. Strong of head and brave into battle! I go onward with my handful of lavender flowers! They are purple and wilting but they are beautiful and marvelous! We go marching into battle! I keep trying to scream and grunt like the others. Grunt grunt scream and grunt like the others. The guy behind me meets with invisible enemy forces. Suddenly he is writhing on stabbing beds of nails and blood from a busted hydrant spurting all over and the most horrible killing sounds. Urga darka loogra! Urga most loogra! Flying sounds blindly through the air all around my elfin ears! I think I can make these sounds but I am not very good at it at all. Urga Durga Urk Ruk Irka Luck! Urga Durga! My hot little head! My tiny tender stomach! Lemon Drops! Crying Pez! And then all the men fight on and we return to the director of the play and he compliments all of the tall grunting men but he doesn't even look at me. He turns his head around and around in all the other directions but he doesn't even see me. I feel like a thin piece of air. Finally he glares at me and hurls insults from the podium while talking into his phone! Even though I was brave enough to go strong of head into battle with my lavender! I start thinking to myself how I can't do anything right. I am only trying to be a good actress but I just can't get it right. Nothing is right.

# ANYWAYS

I say.
Go and love. Anyways. Spread Love.
And fuck Juan Carlos King of Spain.
Fuck him in his pants.
Big fat elephant killer.
How could he?

# MR. BINGO

Mr. Bingo won the lottery! He wasn't much good at anything else, but he knew how to buy tickets. He had a special system. Monday to the Belltown 7-11. Tuesday to the "Thank you very much" store owned by Mr. Koko from the Philippines. The reason Mr. Bingo called it the "Thank you very much" store is because Mr. Koko would always nod and say "Thank you very much, thank you very much!" to everyone, no matter what they bought. No matter if you were in a big bad mood. No matter if you were mean. Mr. Koko also had a free bowl of Bubblicious bubble gum by the door and Mr. Bingo would happily help himself to a handful. Mr. Bingo would travel to different convenience stores every day to buy himself one lone ticket. On Monday morning he would spread out his unique divination system. A deck of cards, set of dominoes, dice. Each week he would plot a different trajectory, every dice and domino representing a different store and location. This Monday he was to go to Foster's Mini-Mart, Tuesday to Frosty's Master Mini Smart-Mart, Wednesday to Big O Jelly George's, run by his friend George. The deck of cards would dictate a specific set of hand gestures that had to be performed to the tune of "It had to be you." Finally he would toss the cards up into the air to conjure up the winning numbers for each day. He would write them down onto a pad of paper with a pen that had thick and sparkly blue ink, like the color of the midnight sky. He would bring the note pad with him to the stores and slowly read the numbers out loud to George and Mr. Koko and Mrs. Foster. He would howl out the numbers like songs to dusty store shelves, like prayers to bring forth his long harbored dreams. He would perfume the air with numbers. "5, 11, 22, 74, 00, 13." In fact these turned out to be his lucky numbers. He won the lottery on Tuesday, July 31, 1995 at Frosty's Master Mini Smart-Mart. He won 6,800 dollars (some of which went to taxes). Mr. Bingo was so happy and picked flowers and handed them out to all the people that came into the store. He stayed all day long. He did a little tango with himself and his face glowed. His hips swayed and he danced as though he was dancing with two of himself. Jelly George and Mr. Koko and Frosty and Mrs. Foster came by and they all celebrated Mr. Bingo's great good fortune.

# DEAD ANGELS

"All the people I've slept with are dead," she stammers, holding her red vinyl purse, hands uncontrollably rattling. "I don't know. I think five, or ten, or twenty. They're all gone, I know they are. Whenever I try to call them they won't pick up." The officer glares at Frances, asks for her drivers license, stares at her photo, wonders how she wound up in Las Vegas, points his eyes up to the sky and asks his next question. "You said you're an angel. Well what does this have to do with the people you've slept with?" "I am an angel. I fly in, take off my dress, wrap my white scarf around them. They get to see my white angel wings for a magical moment. I sleep with them and then they die. All of them, officer." "Well I don't get it. We're going to have to take you in for questioning." "I was doing them a favor, officer." she offers. Surprised, he pulls out his pen and pad to take notes.

"I am doing them a favor. They sleep with the angel of death, these sinners and holy rollers. You can still see the blinking lights reflected in their eyes. The dollar signs, the cherries and plums and oranges and bananas. They're dingers on parade. Sleepwalkers pulling handles, they wait for the rush of gold. Oh the horrible guilt they feel. You have no idea. And their families hate them. They've lost their families. They've lost everything. And then they come to me. My place is next to the Elvis chapel where you can get Elvis to marry you. My place is painted virgin white on the outside but when they come in the door, everything is painted black. And then I appear through a fog of dry ice, naked except for my gigantic white angel wings. It suits me. And then they pay me $4000 to have sex with them. Once they're taken by that mood it's easy to get them to confess their sins. I listen, sometimes for hours. I put my angel wings on their backs and take a photo. Put my arms around them. Hold them until every last speck of guilt is gone. I make sure that every last tinge of guilt is gone. I offer to send a letter of redemption to their families. Then I feed them little pink pills, one by one, like a sacrament. Like Jesus wafers. Their heads are tilted back. My hand softly strokes their hair and I kiss their foreheads. I whisper in their ears that all is forgiven. All is forgiven! And then the organ player starts playing well he's just my friend Dirk. And then they all die. All of them. Usually within minutes. And then I drag them to the back and Dirk takes them to the pit and buries them. It's all good. I'm providing an important service. You know it's all God's work. Yes I know it's God's work."

## JEANINE DIDN'T WANT TO ADD
## ONE MORE SOUND TO THE WORLD

Out stepped Jeanine. Out into the street after slamming her car door shut. Jeanine. Her upper back jumping from the sound of the slam. Jeanine's right thumb reaching for the lock button on the car's keyless device. Jeanine's sharply manicured thumb about to press down to emit the piercing beep sound that signaled the locking of the doors. She paused though. She could not hit the button. She could not press that button. Because she didn't want to add one more sound to the world. She wondered What will the birds think? She did this for the birds. She didn't want to hurt their ears or obstruct their songs. Obstruct their signals to one another. So Jeanine left her car doors unlocked. She even left the doors of her red Pontiac Bonneville wide open on their hinges and all the baby bird chirps came in. Like waves she loved the chirping sounds of no sound no sound no sound coming through like a whale in the wilderness of junkyard love. No sound no sound no sound she said no sound.

# SING!

"I won't sing," cried the little girl. She was six, maladjusted, refused to pick up her messes, and fought with anyone who looked too long in her direction. On the swing set she would push herself high and flutter-kick her little legs on the way down. Which would knock down the children walking by. Swept off their feet like fresh mown dandelions.

But the one thing she loved to do more than anything else was to sing. Sing on the bus ride home, "Dippy dippy dog!" Sing in the shower, "Blue rats and fat cats!" And to her ham and eggs "Jump hammy jump!" as she'd stab the albumen. Lick her plate clean and smack smack smack.

At least her parents never had to entertain her. Why, this girl could sing a cereal box!

Just trying to talk to her could be impossible. She'd stand with feet planted, hands on hips and chin jutting forward as if to say "What. You want to talk to me?"

Then came the day when the girl's second-grade teacher decided to put on a recital for all the parents. The girl was asked to sing, of course. The teacher asked the girl to sing "Joy to the World" and the girl said no. She refused. It was then that she actually spoke the word "No" for the first time. "No, I won't sing!" cried the little girl. "No, I won't sing!"

# MARY AND AMY

Mary blurted Well you aren't going to hear her sing very often so get it while you can. It's a rare thing to hear her sing so you're all lucky she said she would sing for you right now. Mary had been following Amy and her singing. The famous visiting teacher had asked Amy to sing one song for the class and Amy rose hesitantly out of her seat, wincing like she was about to be axed at the guillotine.

She sings like a bird in the tree, whispered Mary with tears in her eyes.

She sings like a bird in the tree.

Amy inched her way forward and stood directly in front of the teacher. She began to sing, quietly and with her head down at first but by the end of her song she was loud with her throat open and head held back with new words sung out like a field of fresh wonder in summer. The teacher was stunned by her song for a quick moment but that didn't last too long because he was more interested in himself because he was the famous teacher after all and his words were like stale crunchy bread but everyone would say Yum! Such soft fresh bread! After all these years he still sang out those old dead words and the students limped after him, feigning interest in his droppings and recording his recommendations in thick pencil lead. But in the end it was the other students who had really heard Amy's song. It was the others who needed her voice for she was just like them. She was just finding her way to her voice and she was a little bit ahead of all the others so she could lead them out into the grassy open field of awe. (The truth is she was just a little less afraid!) The other students followed Amy after class. Followed her down hallways and to the bathroom and followed her around to the foyer. They followed her like dogs tracking a scent and they cornered her, circled her. Asked her When are you going to sing again? Where are you going to sing and could we be there to hear it and where did you learn to sing like that? They wanted to know and her advice to them was this:

You are a voice in the world.

Be like a football player.

Don't give up. Don't give up.

Please.

Don't give up.

# A MOVIE THAT BILL WOULD LIKE TO SEE MADE

A situation came about whereupon there was a writer sitting in a café, twiddling his thumbs, unable to write.

Barely able to move his pen, it dawned on him that he would compose a Great American Novel that would take place solely in someone's basement.

Desperately trying to utilize his last moments on earth in an attempt to write said novel, he complains suddenly of a strained wrist.

Geometric shapes, side of window, lost in time and space, he glances out.

Effort only gains momentum after one has left the moment behind, handlebars free, gliding through the space of an open window.

Frankly, there could be no real use in this. It's just not feasible.

God only knows the price we pay for such innocence. Such aching dreams. Such lofty hopes. Peddling nowhere.

Henry, who happens to be a cloud, is moving fast, frying some scrambled eggs in the sky. He says he is actually a visitor from another planet.

I believe him.

Just then a knock on the door, and in walks Squirrel, hiding from the local Dog who has it in for him. "Do you mind if I stay awhile?" Squirrel chirps breathlessly.

"Kindly." Being the kind Chap I am, I swiftly tumble-down a blanket from the closet and make a cozy little bed in a box. "Here Squirrel, make yourself at home."

"Like I'm going to trust you!" Squirrel says. "Maybe you'll carve me up for dinner!"

"Maybe I'll carve you up, or maybe we'll become great friends and happy neighbors."

"Nice try." says Squirrel. "It's a trap."

"Open your mouth then, Squirrel, and I will crawl in!" cried the Chap, trying not to laugh.

"Perhaps you'd be so kind to at least let me use your bathroom. The Dog has passed by and I best be on my way. I just don't want to leave a scent, if you know what I mean."

"Every question is answered here, dear Squirrel." said the Chap. "The door is open, down the hall to the left. The seat needs lifting then it's all yours."

"Right then." said Squirrel, hopefully anticipating relief in the bladder area.

"Trust is not my forte." cried Squirrel, who waddled half amiably down the hallway and swung the door shut. "I won't be long."

"Under the sink is an extra bar of soap if you need it." said the Chap.

"Very good!" cried Squirrel, and a whizzing sound emanated followed by the glugging sound of a flush.

"Why don't you stop by again sometime?" said the Chap.

"X marks the spot," said Squirrel, who had just finished washing and drying his paws and was now squiddling back down the hallway.

"Yes I think I will if you don't mind. It's a jungle out there."

Just then the cloud named Henry zoomed in through an open window and lifted little squirrel up to the sky.

"Bye bye." they all said. "Bye bye!"

Back in the cafe, all was quiet except for the grating sound of the espresso machine. The great American novel still sadly, unwritten. The writer barely able to move his pen.

# NO WARNING

I was there during the earthquake, when big fat farms moved and grown men's knees buckled to the ground. Cats ran in crazy circles to finally settle under a desk or kitchen table. I was there and watched as haywire walls writhed back and forth, bolts of lightening hit brick buildings and blew them up. No warning.

Earthquakes have a habit of striking out from nowhere, only a distant roar precedes their arrival. And like a dinosaur dancing freakishly on a dining room table, what is large is made to seem impossibly small. And excuse me but Why is there a dinosaur on the dining room table?

I was there during the earthquake, my hands gripping the shaking left and right between the door jamb. In the jaws of a dog ripping a squirrel to pieces. The ripping lasts a long time, longer than it would take to normally kill a squirrel. The dog shakes its prey on and on for no good reason on and on.

After the quake all the floors became moving skateboards, a treachery. I keep my eye on the front door, moving gingerly, one foot after another like a geisha so as not to disturb the wounded scenery. Flip flop life, vase of flowers upside down and a towering ear canal silence, reverberating. Distant siren draws too close. Car door slams, someone laughs next door like a welcome angel. Says "Well that wasn't too bad." Someone is shaking and the cat's eyes are dark and far off with fear, his tiny solar plexus tight and huddled back onto his haunches.

# DAVID

I first met David in a toy store where I had gone in search of a shiny new Duncan Imperial Spintastic Dragonfly Yoyo for my nephew Louis. I bumped into David repeatedly in the aisles and remember being curious about his charmingly boy-ish manner. He was acting like an annoying teenager, playing with bouncing balls and showing off and talking non-stop. He was talking in this kind of baby language and I thought, Oh this kind of guy is fun. Then he offered to take me out to lunch at a shop call "Stuff-Its" where he paid for my meal in pennies and quarters, and that took like 20 minutes. Then during lunch he affectionately dubbed me Cyclops because my bangs completely covered one of my eyes. He stared deeply into my one eye like I was really someone special and leaned in while absently dropping his elbow into his plate of Stuff-Its sandwich. His elbow got covered in a thick coat of mayonnaise and avocado, which he tried to lick off but he couldn't reach his elbow with his tongue.

David and I were to be married in a friend's backyard in Sebastopol. He had proposed to me in a romantic fast-food sushi restaurant that sort of felt like a McDonalds. The rice in the sushi was hard and chewy like a real McDonald's hash-brown patty, because the cooks have to race around so fast that they don't have time to cook the rice all the way through. The walls are painted firestorm red and there are fallen bits of seaweed, sushi rice and ginger all over the floors. When you leave you have to wipe your sticky shoes off in the grassy poopy dog area outside. Ginger and poop scattered everywhere.

Instead of giving me a ring David gave me a tattered red velvet box and in it was a small plastic cow. He said, Sister, will you marry me? Earlier he had excitedly placed little hints in the house. Plastic pigs had fallen from kitchen cupboards. Plastic chickens had been falling out of boxes of tea. Plastic penguins poked their heads from under bed pillows and plastic tigers perched precariously on doorknobs and toilet seats. I said yes.

## THE WEDDING

It was our summer wedding day and I had invited all of our friends because David wasn't really capable of inviting them. We hadn't even figured out what we were going to wear. The whole thing was haphazard and lacking in any ritual, unlike the ritualized performance art pieces David was so famous for. David told me I should wear something that poofed out like a tutu and I thought, Well, I do have the dress I wore for my friend Sharonda's wedding. I could wear that. I started to think about how David didn't really care about these sorts of things and so I decided to call my father, who, for some strange reason, wasn't going to be attending the wedding anyways, so I thought of him as an unbiased observer. The wedding was just hours away and all of our friends had driven from San Francisco to Sebastopol and had parked and were now walking toward the backyard where the wedding was to take place. Even the orange cat was walking down to the backyard from the main house where he usually slept in a basket.

After I spoke with my father I decided to call the whole thing off. It dawned on me that none of this seemed quite right and it was the first time I had realized this, even though I had almost kicked the stuffing out of David in his van at Theater Grotowski after I found out that he had slept with yet another of my so-called good friends. I went straight in with swift kicks to the shins. If it weren't for his big smelly friends holding me back by the arms, why I think I would have killed him. I resorted to karate kicking the sides of the van so hard that the whole van started to rock uncontrollably. I am sure it looked to passers-by like a huge blob of people were having horrible violent sex in a giant tin can.

Anyways, after I called the whole thing off, I was sitting under the big willow tree where we were supposed to be married. I was sitting with the orange cat and we were meowing at each other sweetly and sometimes even in unison. Suddenly two Native American guys from down the street opened the gate to the yard. I liked the sound of the green grass crunching under their feet. I admired their hoop earrings and they said they knew all about my future and they said it was all cool. It would all be fine. One of them laughed and told me that I shine like a penny in the sun or like a quarter on the subway.

We all sat together under the tree for quite some time and we didn't say much more. We were comfortable just being quiet. Then I thanked them and they left and we waved goodbye. Then the two of them went to see David up in the main house and they offered him smoke and sugar water.

Then        they burned        the hair        from his arms.

## THE SPACESHIPS

That night I saw a ton of spaceships in the sky. The orange cat that was supposed to be in the wedding was staring up

into the sky and he was naming them. He seemed to know
their names and from which planet every spaceship was from.
Urgulmalure.    Belanchet. Seesawton.         Ooshamaloo-
sha.  Cumsersidaddle.    Elastica. Bombardica.
Losta Ma Loosa Mon.


It all—the sounds of the words and the—it all sounded
like the—
and
the ships like a fire in the heavens – like   a fire in the
heavens—like the—like
the
weirdest-sounding foreign language—and it was. It was—
So
beautiful.


The cat and I stayed up all night meowing, listening to music
and choreographing ice skating routines, doing waltz jumps
through the air. Meowing.    Softly.

# FATHER RAWLINGS

Father Rawlings is clearly a sex addict masquerading as a yoga teacher. His advice to the class is this: The posture of Vandana-Schtupya should feel mmmm mmm good. Like I'm licking ice cream off your body! I found this advice, as well as the posture, to be a bit of a red flag.

At the end of the class we all have to do a group hug. All the students are female and the only man is Father Rawlings and he happens to put himself conveniently in the center of the group hug and I notice all the other women are sort of writhing around him and he has this huge grin on his face. He says I feel like a rock star like Jim Morrison. He shouts with a big smile. I am Jim Morrison the yoga instructor! He even has hair like Jim Morrison (though it's a bit shorter but he even has a square jaw like Jim.)

From the center of the writhing circle I can feel everyone inside of me like jelly. The fridge makes ticking sounds all night. I can't leave this French room. I am covered in black lace and I am a tourniquet. He is the size of a football. I could try to do a ritual where I pray over my no longer hated body. I could try to breathe the way I want to, but I can't. I just can't breathe. This time I throw a firebomb into the crowd. The police chase me. I go to confession and throw a stone through the grates of the priest's black box and it lands deep on the ocean floor. I broadcast my voice and it is one big open window and the salt air keeps pouring in. Groups of seagulls are listening, swift and undying into the night.

## NIGHT

And then if you try to get away from the group hug Father Rawlings says You ugly old hag! And then he grabs your hair by the roots and rips it out. Seriously! Chunks of it with bloody skin!

And then he says the hair pull is actually a secret yoga posture called The Lumpenzviegen that brings healthy circulation to the roots and helps grow shiny new buoyant hair.

He says it is best to do the Schtupya posture before the Lumpenzviegen. Or even better to do the Schtupya and Lumpenzviegen together—performing them at the same time.

And then after the group hug the teacher picks out one special student and they sit on meditation cushions and stare into each other's eyes for a long time until the whole world becomes a circle. At this point he doesn't even try to make people pay the $25 for class because he is so focused on staring into the special student's eyes.

Today her name is Ashley and she's writhing around like an aerial circus performer. He gives her a spiky rose quartz crystal the size of an egg and she slowly places it under her butt. Sits down on top of it on the floor and writhes. She trembles and moans on top of the rose quartz. She wants everyone to see what is sexy. Then they play Doctor and the Doctor won't leave my bedroom and he just keeps staring over at me with his drippy cloud face and dreamy eyes. And all the other students feel just horrible about themselves. They feel as big as a smushed fly, but like a fly they keep coming back class after class. There is jealousy smeared everywhere. Jealousy smeared like rotten yellow eggs on old walls and it's running out of the over-flowing toilet, a dark liquid. Old musty sex-smelling bed clothes smeared with jealousy. The unwashed hair of a 26-year-old sticking straight up. Everyone can hear the love-making through the walls. The yipping. The screaming and endless moaning! She walks out of the bedroom with raccoon mascara eyes. Cold cup of coffee in her hand. Shaking. He roasts a clove of garlic on the open kitchen gas flame while his girlfriend watches. He peels it and plops it into her open mouth. He says women are like mushy escargot. They get blackened and grilled over an open fire and then eaten like a piece of sushi and then their bellies are nibbled apart and you can see confetti in their underwear or sometimes they're not even wearing underwear. Their bodies are dirty. They're like little girls not even grown up yet and they're wearing baggy white underwear that's just far too big for them. They wear only one pair of dirty stretched out white underwear because their mothers have neglected them. Nobody ever comes to help them when they scream out into the dark night.

## BIRD FLIES OUT OF THE DARK NIGHT

It's winter at the Macy's Day Parade. She's happily sitting on the edge of a cement wall, kicking her dangling legs and watching all the elephants and grandmothers do a slow walk by. They sway and wave and saunter. All of their hips are especially prominent. Popcorn springs up through the crowd, hitting heads and upturned mouths and a whole lot of crunching goes on. Father Rawlings appears like a beacon through one of the marching bands. Dressed in a tie-dyed hot pink tee shirt and baggy green cargo pants and sandals.

One arm stretched enthusiastically up in the air, smiling toward her. Father Rawlings bows and gifts her with the tell-tale plum-sized pale pink rose quartz tetrahedra. She bows toward Father Rawling's big eyes and slowly places the crystal under her butt. She trembles and moans as she writhes on top of it. She wants everyone in the parade to see what is sexy. Then they play Doctor and the Doctor won't leave my bedroom and he just keeps staring over at me with his drippy cloud face and dreamy eyes.

Look! The witch is there in the parade, too!

## THE WITCH

takes back her cape
pulls it toward her     Twists it    and pulls it    toward
her                 reveals
the  Secret   Night  of   Snow    Hears  a soft    flut-
ter  of wings   Turns her head   to listen   Lets her robe
slide    down to the floor   It gathers   around her twisted
feet       Lets her robes fall
all     her robes      fall    fall
Soundless    In the
light     of     the
moon    the moon   So    So    still
Reveals her skin and body       her face and
         her    and  her big tits   (What? Did I
         write that?)
The witch takes back the night.    She slowly
  lets her robe      fall     to the floor    where it
        gathers in a soft pile   around      her
        twisted feet. She lets her robes fall    all
        her robes fall   fall    in the moonlight

to reveal                           the glow of her
body and her luminous face.            She
turns            around and around            in
little circles       turns     around and around
her                                          self
                                    turns around.

# BONANZA YELLING OUT HER SPEECH IN THE AUDITORIUM

Piles and piles of girls wake up! Drag yourselves up from the dirt and manure! Zombies crossing the road wake up! There has never been anything wrong with you. Girls. With your little wigs and heads bobbing. Girls. With that lost look in your eyes. Girls. Buried in piles of dirt and stink. There has never been anything wrong with you! Girls. You are now waking up! I command you get up! Not a single one of you will be left behind! Lori Fred the Beast wake up! Amber Ocean with the Amazing Marble Brown Eyes get up! And get up Lori Fred! Get up onto your weak little horse legs! Shake off that clotted dirt and arise! Little Limp Suzette. Astrid. Lingafore. Penitence. Rye Bread. Marmalade. Arise you Ancient Ones Arise. You!     There is nothing     wrong        with you! There          has never been       anything           wrong with       you.

## POET ROBERT LOWELL'S HIGH SCHOOL COMMENCEMENT SPEECH IN THE AUDITORIUM

Robert Lowell became quite swelled up in body. Robert Lowell was a half real and half fake mannequin. Sometimes he was half a cloud and half a ghost. He lifted his arms and steadied himself on the old oak log. His body was cloaked in his musty graduation gown. Its loose butterfly-shaped arms swung around and around him and his booming voice spoke like Moses on the top of the station of the cross. Yonder thou shalt not! He said. Though yonder thou shalt become guides to the sanctuary. Then Robert Lowell hardened into a tree that the people came to talk under and they sat in his arms and wrapped their legs tight around his swinging boughs. Mostly they made love under the tree and tossed orange peels in springtime.

# THE DEE DEE STORY

The writer thinks he may have written an important story called <u>Dee Dee's Big Black Eyelash</u> but he's troubled because he can't remember writing it.

The writer says to himself      I'm afraid of my imagination it's chasing me and then I'm imagining my imagination is going to git me         or my imagination is imagining gitting me        or imagining that I'm imagining me gitting me.

He found the crumpled story typed onto a piece of letter paper, stacked in an old wicker basket in his study. It was buried under a box of Kleenex, tax papers and battered old journals. When he found it he was baffled. Was he the author? The Dee Dee story was not a journalistic piece, for sure, but it was about somebody. It was about a person named Dee Dee who has a dog and it is about where she lives and what she looks like and that's about it. The writer thinks he slightly remembers writing it, maybe in that dark purple motel room the night he got beat up. But he wasn't drunk. He certainly wasn't drunk. So he feels like he would remember more details if he really did write it. It's disturbing to him, this lack of memory.

The writer says to himself      I'm afraid of my imagination it's chasing me and then I'm imagining my imagination is going to git

Upon reading the Dee Dee story he feels like he would write a sentence like "whirl you like churned butter" but still he's not sure if he really would say that in the context of a story about a person named Dee Dee. He might say something like "fur in her ears" but he's not sure he would know anything about how often an SSI check would arrive. (He questions the overall accuracy of the piece and even the grammar. He can tell that it has not yet been edited.)

Though ashamed to admit it, the writer is deathly afraid the police will come to his house and try to arrest him for stealing some other writer's words. The very thought of it turns his skin a whitish grey. His teeth start chattering on their own! He hopes that perhaps the real author will come forward to claim this story of Dee Dee so he doesn't get thrown in jail. He would like to know for sure that he did not steal these words. This would give him great peace of mind. And great peace of mind is something he would like to have even more than writing an important piece like the Dee Dee Story.

For a moment he thinks maybe he really should be sent to jail where he could await trial while quietly meditating in his cell. He would sit cross-legged in his underwear on the cold cement floor and grow a stinky beard and concentrate on attaining great peace of mind. And maybe he would even find it.

it's chasing me and then I'm imagining my imagination is gitting git gittin git!

But perhaps the real author of the Dee Dee Story would so kindly come forward and make an appearance on the local evening news? The desperate author would appear on the screen, his hair greased back and his face a foody mess. Like he hadn't washed in days. Like he had been looking for Dee

Dee for years. He would be wearing big black bifocals, lime green shorts and a shirt the color of a piece of lemon Fruit Stripe gum. He would speak to the newscaster in a nervous stutter. He would say I, I, I'm sorry, but I seem to have lost my Dee Dee story. It's about Dee Dee's big black eyelash and that's pretty much it. The reporter's eyes would turn down in pity, and then he would deliver his plea deep into the camera lens. He would say For Pete's sake if someone there has this man's story, please come forward! For cryin' out loud please call the station!

**And the Phone Number is....**
And the phone number would roll silently across a blank screen for maybe five minutes.

Or maybe the real author would rent a billboard. On it would be an image of a shrouded man hunched and weeping and the word balloon would say Have you seen my Dee Dee Oh?

The writer, in desperation, decides to go door to door to ask the neighbors if any of them had known a person named "Dee Dee." His words would be cryptic, because he wouldn't want yet someone else to steal the Dee Dee story!

But the writer doesn't go door to door. He doesn't have the nerve.

## HIS HAIR

Instead, the writer begins to worry so much about being arrested that he starts to lose his mousy brown hair. Pieces of it falling in short clumps all over the floor in the kitchen, bedroom, bathroom, and staircase. The writer begins to stay up all night, wondering if any of his words have ever been really his? He gets up at night for a snack and trips down the stairs on his fine slippery hair. Slides all over the floor and falls down and hits his head. Again! Blood and hair fill his soft puffy mouth. His nose pressed hard and sideways into the floor. Which makes him drool into an ever-widening puddle.

## THE EPIPHANY

He has the thought that maybe all of his stray words should be taken back to the dog pound or the no-kill shelter? Maybe he needs to put all his words in that wicker basket and give them away to strangers and children? He would do this and there would be nothing left of him except his hat. Yes, he would become just his most prized hat, sitting on his living room couch. His blood and fallen hair would be all around the floor in the living room and his Ferrecci Men's white wool bowler hat would sit peacefully on the couch. The hat he used to wear out when he would go to the soiree where he would pretend he was a writer. At the soiree where he'd wear his big brown buck shoes.

(He could often be seen at the soiree slouching at the food table, stocking up for nourishment on celery stuffed with cream cheese, those tiny caved-in bran muffins, and deviled eggs. His right big buck shoe would make a conspicuous flapping sound as he crossed the room. Slap tap tap as the sole was starting to come off the shoe and he couldn't fix it. He had no money for shoe glue!)

The writer says to himself   I'm imagining me gitting me imaginin in in in.

That's it. The detectives would arrive and the only clues to his disappearance would be the Dee Dee story, the hat and the bloody hair on the floor. Maybe there wouldn't even be a Dee Dee story. He would have burned it.

Look! Oh my God! It's the real Dee Dee story!

## DEE DEE'S BIG BLACK EYELASH

"Dawn hit the edge of Dee Dee's big black eyelashes with a bang. Dee Dee was an allergic girl, timid, yet sexual. She rarely went out of her house, and received her SSI check bi-monthly. Her SF apt. was on the lowest floor, slightly dank, and if you entered her apt. you would enter the world of Dee Dee. Greeted by her child-eyed dog Pissy, a bishon, you would be battered by rough growls and Pissy chasing his tail in circles that would whirl you like churned butter. Dee Dee wore only one red ruffled dress, chiffon, with a stain, from the thrift shop on Hay Street. Dee Dee was a lady who had short blond fur that grew on the sides of her face and if you looked close enough, you would see large pores, edgy lines, even fur in her human ears."

## ROBERT LOWELL SAYS

*"Yet why not say what happened?"*
-Robert Lowell

# A LITTLE LEARNING
# IS A DANGEROUS THING

Two weeks ago, fifteen boys and girls from Longham's Castro High School lined up to be shot by the firing squad, their knees quivering like tinkering piano keys. They had all gotten less than favorable scores on their GRE exam. After all those years of study. Bang. Shot dead. This past week's celebrity firing squad shot dead a row of ten lively girls from the Beaumont School who had scored too low on their S.A.T.'s. Well, today we'll see about the next batch. The I.Q. test is harder to judge as it's a wee bit more subjective, but nonetheless punishable by death if one is to fail.

Fourteen five-year-olds sit drooling and pulling their fingers from their mouths. One is autistic and not afraid of anything. One is shy and still pees his pants. Today's I.Q. test is administered by our special guest star Miss Anna Freud, the sixth and last child of Sigmund and Martha Freud. Anna sits in the corner of the kindergarten and holds a golden stopwatch while calling out in her husky voice, "Go" and "Stop" and "Next section" and "Turn the page yah."

Sigmund would have been proud that none of the children in this batch had yet ripped up their exams in frustration or called out for their mothers. This batch might well succeed in not failing at all. This batch might be spared.

Little Jennifer twirls her number two pencil, eyes dim and laced with worry. They had taught her in school that the sky was blue, though in her little mind's eye the sky was full of crazy colors, colors that only she could name, and she named them names like Peppy, Pop-a-lot, Squirmy, and Fleshy. She hadn't had the nerve to tell anyone about these colors much less the pages of the I.Q. exam. She dragged her pencil heavily across the page. Clicked off the box for "sky is blue." Anna watches pleased as Jennifer ticks off box after box even though her hand is sweating a bright red from gripping her pencil.

Yah, Anna thought, this batch would not be shot after all. This batch would be spared. She knew her father would be proud to know that a little learning is not such a dangerous thing after all.

Don't let your light dim. Even if your mother told you to put a bag over it.
    —Bonanza—5th grader

## ON THE DAY OF THE FIRING SQUAD

We prepare our children as we would on any other day. They get ready for school with their Prince and Princess lunchboxes packed full of tuna fish sandwiches. We ask them if they've got their homework. We make sure their shoes are tied and their zippers zipped and their sleeves rolled up above their wrists. We make sure they have enough layers. But this day is indeed different from all other days.

This day is different because we have put them in pairs of Administrative issue plastic blue handcuffs. They jerk about like dogs on a chain. Their heads move in half circles and their bodies buck. Then we cast them to the Administers.

Administers drink sweet blue sodas from straws and it colors their teeth and their gums and makes their smiles look like melted popsicles. They wear clean brown suits with pinstripes and tediously oiled leather shoes. They wear their sacks slung diagonally over their shoulders and their posture is proper. In the sacks are the paperkeepings on the children. Years of paperkeepings culminating in the testing. Years of keeping notes on the way red toy trucks glide about through the air in the hands of the little ones. Observing their play as the children run in and out of yellow sunlight.

The Selected clutch their handcuffed hands to their home-work as they are taken to school that day, even though they're not going to need it anymore. The older ones know better and toss their papers to the wind.

The families reach the courtyard of the school. They all stand together looking up at the tall flight of stairs that leads to the front lobby where they will check in with the Administers one final time. They had all gotten their notices of the impending squad firing ceremony and were required to arrive at 7 am.

The children on the list begin to speak. First softly and then with voices rising. They always say things like this even though no one is listening;

I want to go on! Let me live! Isn't it enough that I'm just alive? Look at my shoes and shoelaces and look at how my hair is tousled! What do you want me to do? I'll do it! Just let me live and I'll go live in a cave or a garage or behind the school! Isn't it enough that I'm alive? Look at me! I'm alive I'm alive! Momma, Papa, I'm alive! Why did you ever even born us?

But this is just their day, just another day on the line. The parents are prepared for this possibility from the moment they conceive their children. If the children do not perform well on the tests they know the consequences. The parents prepare to be instant empty nesters. Most of them buy tickets for the seashore. They commence their vacation immediately after the firing. They run to their cars as quickly as they can, bags packed and ready to go.

The children who were not the Selected that day proceed to build wet clay replicas of each of the lost children. The replicas are set out in a section of the courtyard called The Cement-ary. Every year on the anniversary of the date of the firing, the families of the children go to the Cement-ary to dress the statues in their dead children's clothing. They paint the girl's lips and nails a stark red. H&M tee-shirts and accessories. Red blush on their cheeks and blue jeans from the Gap. I-pods strapped around their ears with the children's favorite music blasting.

There are the packs of Unselected children known as "The children who make it through." The brains in their heads seem to be expanded like a large full stomach, what with their above average test scores. They become torturous hall monitors when the Administers have too much to do. Sunila Rogan, with tiny upturned nose, was one of them. Mousy brown hair, fast-talking with plaid green skirt, white turtleneck, suspenders and greasy skin. She had always been hard to understand, but now that she was a hall monitor, it was even harder to understand her. She specifically chose the most sophisticated words and she spoke very quickly. Some of the students had taken to carrying dictionaries with them to look up the words of Sunila. The words that seemed like they would be most important to know because they might be on a test. Their very lives could depend upon this important information.

# MR. ULMER WILLIAM MAZEWELL

Mr. Ulmer Mazewell sat in his big frumpy chair with swollen hands, puffing and patting his papers. Stacks and stacks of SAT test scores at his fingertips. He worked hard for the HG Corporation. He would set his black digital timer for each student review. Perfectly clocking 60 seconds. Huffing and puffing through the files as if he were a small child racing through autumn leaves. He liked to challenge himself with speed. Today's first 60 second decision went like this:

Edwin Mathes. Graduates in 2014. Loves hayrides, soccer and all-beef patties etc. Edwin is a very important person to his grandmother in that he helps her on Saturdays with the grocery shopping. He also helps her get up and down the stairs every day. SAT test scores: below average.

Mr. Mazewell makes his split second decision and enthusiastically stamps "DEATH SQUAD" on Edwin's file! His hand flies high into the air and the stamp comes down with a bouncy thump. These scores will never do and we've always got to clean house, yep clean up the house, spits Ulmer. He is almost singing, as the black mole on the side of his mouth moves up and down and up and down with his jiggly smile.

Mr. Mazewell is particularly pleased that Edwin, with his soccer player body, has been feasting on all-beef patties, fries, milkshakes and the like. Ulmer quite contentedly drools at the added bonus of a healthy, supple and rippling "Steak de Edwin." This new tender meat would make his week. His lightly sodden liver and other organs would be an amazing added delight, just like having dessert, he thinks. He salivates as he thinks of Ed's ruddy big boy cheeks. Ulmer's eyes look gratefully up to his God in the sky.

You see, the only nutrition Mr. Mazewell is able to absorb is that of human meat. In fact most of the Administers are like him. Over the last five years, most of them have been diagnosed with a mysterious blood disorder called Likenstumps. Their system rejects the standard vegetable, cow meat, fish, chicken, lamb, corn, wheat and even delicious desserts. Indeed, they are driven to eat their own. Think of it – it is like these children are their own! You know, there's nothing like a living, breathing, functional school system! Others across the globe take note! Teachers around the world take heed! Listen up! Heads up from your desks! Here in the town of Longham, everyone pitches in and everyone helps everyone else! Every school system should be so caring and loving. Good schools set the tone for future generations. Good schools raise up good, conscientious adults. In good schools, ethics is number one. And thank God for the highly rational meter of test scores. If it weren't for the SAT's what ever would they do? How would they decide who has to go? Someone has got to go. The Administers have a right to live too!

**There is a current theory that proposes the following:**

New diseases (like Likenstumps) are born for a reason. For example, the emotional over-flooding of the feeling of shame causes the body's cells to mutate and twist upward in a helical fashion. This mutant response creates the disease, but the disease in turn actually allows the person to overcome the discomfort of the original feeling (of shame.) Through inheriting the disease, the original feeling is, in fact, totally and completely erased. In this way, the disease is beneficial to the organism, and to society as a whole. As in this example, shame is erased, and entire families can live a peaceful and stress-free existence.

And besides, it would be wasteful for the Administers to execute the children and not eat their bodies. Years ago they would just throw them in the dump. Likenstumps keeps down food waste.

# BRAINS

When I discovered I was lied to, that I wasn't a brilliant person as a child, that I was only a normal child with a normal set of brains, I wanted to do something about it. I decided I would figure out a way to get more brains, and at the cost of sounding vain I knew that I had a right to steal the brains if I wanted to. So I set out on my life path to become a scientist. I would research the brains of smart people and I would reach my hands into their greasy grey matter and figure out how to inject it into myself. As I grew smarter and smarter, my head grew bigger and I wanted to pound my way into all the heads on earth so that my head would be the biggest head and no one could lie to me anymore about how smart I am. Because I am very smart. Yes I am!

## THE WRITER SAYS

You can't steal my words and you can't take my voice even though I have to pay for the right to it by my education and precision, refinement, time to study and pay the bills.

–The Writer

# ROBBY

Robert Lowell admits he was a beast who drowned kittens and now he says he wants to apologize. Also for all the beatings and all the drunkenness.

You beast you. Fuck you Robert Lowell once and for all. And who cares if you won an Emmy?

To take away is
to take away.

Nothing from nothing
leaves nothing.
Leaves, all leaves.
All autumn leaves
blowing away.
Away.

# ROBERT LOWELL'S BROTHER LINT LOWELL
## APPLIES TO COLLEGE TOO

And thi

And this

is his application to college:

(Please read!) (Stupid!) :

(Hush! Due to your own very special specialness, YOU are now made privy to my top-secret high security admissions application to a very influential MFA Creative Writing Program, located somewhere (I can't say) in or around London, England.)

(Rustling papers.)

"300-500 words concerning your purpose for undertaking graduate study your reasons for wanting to study your research interests professional plans career goals. You may also want to explain your..."

(Ahem. Throat clearing.)

Dear Mr. and Mrs. School Monger,

I am an important figure in the history of writing here in the United Republic of the State of a large swimming pool. Anyways – I WILL be a very important figure in literature, especially after the hurricanes hit and all the people on earth are gone.

My purpose here on earth is to get through writing this application. I am very happy to provide you with recommendations from people who think I am wonderful and you can talk to them about the reasons you should hire me as a student into your gracious program. I am like a genious or something. You should recognize me as gifted and special and like the second coming of Hans Christian Winston Salem the 3rd, because I am, Hans Christian Winston Salem the 3rd. (You can also call me Lint.)

In answer to your questions, my favorite color is green but really my favorite color is blue sometimes. (I imagine that Miss America will be taking notes.)

I like to win any game and if I don't, I get mad. I like to take my writing very seriously and never have any fun at writing because writing IS very serious. It is like throwing knives and spears or really it is war. Gladiators dust off their suits and throw globs of words. Bloody messy words fight over the best word. Shredded headless words roll around on top of one another, moaning. Dead words lie in a bloody pile on the ground, teeming with maggots! All this writing is like conscription and signing up for this life where you never have any time to just sit down and eat, or something.

I appreciate your consideration, and if you do not accept me I will be heart-broken and then I will get a job at a hospital where I will take my dog around so he can meet people and I will rub the people's feet and put on a big red nose and act like a clown. If I don't get a job at a hospital I will take a bushel of apples down the street to the woman who just had twin boys. I will write them a card and take them a bushel of apples. I will still go to war.

Thank you for your lovely interpretation of my application. I believe in you.

Goodbye.

Goodbye again,

And I PROMISE if you accept me I will never eat crunchy chips in class.

But, rest assured, I WILL look over my shoulder and COPY what all the others are writing,

Sincerely,

Mr. Hans Christian Winston Salem 3rd – Proud MFA College Supplicant

(As I told you before, I am also known as Lint Lowell. Robert Lowell's brother.)

# DATELINE BOMBAY

I've walked the muddy streets of Mumbai in a blur, the last monsoon deposited rivers of sewage, cars hoisted up higher than the tops of cow's heads. Water bloating, water receding. I am wearing my usual get-up. I am Gaston, French journalist, originally from Marseilles. Light khaki jacket with lots of pockets, many rooms for cigarettes, bidis they call them here. Crackling Indian snacks and warm sugar candies in another pocket. This is not like New York, back east, the places I now call headquarters. Green marine Salvation Army pants, room for jack knife, small blue notepad, compact purple pen, I can smell melting plastic. The summer heat of Mumbai is of course sweltering and the locals are pushing their way into me, grabbing at shards and targeting me for a sale. Me? For a sale? Dangling whip-like souvenir snakes made of jointed wood, slithering in front of my face and nearly slapping me. They beg me to buy a snake. "Take home for son, take home for son." "What son?" I ask. The snake salesman is skinny, a rail, rags sticking to his faded brown skin, mole on his cheek, one eye looked bad, real bad, like it had been sewn shut through tears. Arms held too close to his body, like an invisible man was hugging him from behind. Snake reaches out to me snapping. I say no, again. Reach for my pack of bidis. Can't find my goddamn lighter. Where the hell was my passport? Warm skin to skin. Honking cars diesel smoke rubbing bodies pushing past me. "Sir, sir, sir, cutlet, cutlet, cutlet" the vendor cries out. Cutlets, flat chickpea patties, fried, with spices. Hot oil up my nose, bidi smoke, I take a drag, another arm with a snake. I'm here to do important work, I tell myself. I am Gaston, French journalist, originally from Marseilles. Another arm with a snake comes swerving at me from a distance. I begin to run. We all begin to run. Hundreds of us. Or hundreds of thousands of us. Here in India you can no longer tell.

# CHEESE

I am afraid of cheeseburgers. No really, the kind that bleed when you squish them between two soft halves of buns. Really, what were they thinking? I'm thinking of the face of a cow, with big round button eyes like saucers with cream. Thinking of all kinds of cows, big milk cows and big Brahman cows. You see, I'm thinking of them, and my name is Jhonni from Jaipur. My name is Jhonni and I am Animal Liberator and it became my cause the day they unveiled the first MacDonald's Walla store in Jaipur. Imagine, in a country that venerates cows, unveiling a golden arched building that fries up the holy remains of cows until they drip with their own fat. Up in smoke they go. This is not the familiar smell of moist chapatti puffing over an open flame. How could this be the honeyed taste of cane juice squeezed fresh on the street? Yes, I am Jhonni, Animal Liberator, and I have come to steal the keys to the MacDonald's Walla cow-killer smoke shack. I will steal the keys and liberate the cows, and if there are no cows alive I will walk their remains straight to Varanasi. I will take the rows and rows of crispy wrapped cheeseburgers sitting under heat lamps and set them on a float in the Mother Ganges, where I will say my prayers and thank the Lord Shiva that at least some of their souls will be saved. It is the very least I could do as a MacDonald's Walla Animal Cheeseburger Liberator. To save the souls of these delicately wrapped cows. The problem right now is my friend Sunil just whispered to me that MacDonald's in India does not serve hamburger it is illegal in India. So my report is incorrect. They do serve Chicken Maharaja-Mac and Spicy Delights BigSpicy Paneer Wrap and Fiery Paneer Punch.

The next problem is my friend Sunil just told me that the Coca-Cola Company now owns the Mother Ganges. Look this up and you too will be outraged!

# MISTER ELEPHANT

In this heat there is nothing left to do but go racing for the riverside! Enough lazing about under Old Grandpa Banyan tree at the famous Hampi Bazaar. I must get up and go! Although getting my twelve thousand pound Elephant Body up in this heat is a hard thing to do! In case you're wondering, I reside in the ancient village of Hampi, India. Hampi gets splitting hot in February! All of the big stones of Hampi look just like me. Huge monumental shades of gray stones jut out of waterways and hillsides. Big stones like whales lying belly-side everywhere! Ah, there it is – the Tungabhadra river! Off in the distance. Here I go! Get out of my way, bicycle! India is far too crowded for Pete's sake! I always hope for not too many children on the seashore. I need my space. I lope along these crazy streets, full of bindi colors and ladies swaddled in thin flowing fabrics. My legs begin to pound the ground like a Bhoomi Dundubhi Drum! My trunk high in the air looks like a gigantic squirming cobra! I am an old and musty Mammoth dinosaur without all that bothersome Wooly! My big ropy tail sticks straight up like a piece of wicker! And look at my regal bindi! Some men have painted a large circle of red on my broad illustrious forehead! Could I be any more handsome? Here I go past zooming taxicabs and smoky street food stands. Auto rickshaws buck and jerk their way down alleyways. Greasy haired men with antiquated mustaches lean on sides of buildings and tourists point and stare. Arms reach out to touch me and I let them. I let them brush by my wrinkled bag of skin. I even let them slap my skin! Slap my wrinkled legs! They look like a huge old Brahmin woman's legs if the wind was to lift up her sari!

Up with the sari and you see the honorable Brahmin woman's funny blue underwear and large ass! Folds of sour smelling flapping leathery fat! Caked splotches of lentil dal! Okay now out of my way! Can't you see I'm sweating! Okay here I come! OOOOhhhhhhhh. I can barely control my walk anymore or my swinging belly. Danger danger. Onto the sand and down the steep dune. Out of my way! I'm an elephant! There's a reason you've made me a Deity here! AHhhhh, okay. I announce my arrival at the waterside! Okay, aren't I the coolest dude on the block. Oh this is going to be good. Here I go! Oh watch the water part for me! The sand the sand the river green river and cool cold cool. Ooooh now I go down like a building capsizing into water! Splash! Now I am a skyscraper pulverizing the vast ocean! Splash! I am the silvery moon fallen! Down down falling freely I cannot control I take the big plunge head up high and then whoosh water in my trunk drinking and twisting as the water cascades down facial arenas and oh the tips of my ears and my hearing acute. Oh, my soft egg-shaped forehead. Whooshing earless sounds so close up right with me. Water water creeping up around my ears. I am water I am water. Beautiful. Below my lugging belly I can feel the sand, the softness. Pressing up against me. Oh I think I'm going to roll! I'm rolling! Oh I'm rolling! And all the people laugh at me for some reason when I roll. Children point and laugh! Can't they see, I am happy! Happy! Happy! I am the Great Mister Elephant of the Tungabhadra shore!

# MISTER ELEPHANT HAS DREAMS

At night I dream of my elephant brothers and sisters with their silver-bodied children, crossing the tundra in the dark. Racing away from the shadows of men with their fast cars and rifles. Legs pounding, legs galloping. Racing away into the cool night air. Covering vast distances. Hearts beating fast and tears pouring from huge almond eyes.
Oh sparkling stars of the sky. Please save our elephants. I beg the stars in the sky. Do my dream bidding.
Or I will become darkness.
My heart is a heavy pile of love.
My heart is a pile of heavy love.
Heavy.
So heavy.
But not hard.

# MISTER ELEPHANT PLAYS A SYMPHONY

Mister Elephant sits in the tall jungle grass, singing and
playing his violin. His head tilts back and his arms swing in
bliss. The people gather round, their hot bodies draped on
rocks, and listen.

**He sings**
Well I don't often get down on my knees
to beg you please
but this night it's me
here in the swings
I need to feel free.
Need to feel free.
All of us
elephants
singing now
buried
and swaying
singing and playing
down under the ground.
Down into the ground.
And all of us
I'm just saying
need to feel free
need to be free.
We need to be free.

# THE WRITER

It has been a long time since the writer has put pen to paper. It is as if he has been possessed of a great flu, or a broken bone, or a kidnapping. Yes, this is more like a kidnapping. He has become, in this fever, nothing like he really is. He has become what one might call a great little ant face. His bigger face in the mirror is nothing more than a gross exaggeration.

It is as though he were a child and the world has shaken the life out of him. Thrown him against walls and broken all his bones. His eyes are dim and old and the operation takes six hours. No one would give him back his life and he roams the streets like this. Limping in his stiff white frock. He used to have a paint-brush in his hand. He used to have a pencil. He used to have his banjo.

Inside the burned out buildings he sees important men shaking hands. Making deals about the lives of fish and silver. Never do they speak about the elephants. Never. But the writer, the writer speaks about the elephants all the time. Elephants, elephants, he says. But still the men they walk over his body and they walk over his giant sword. Elephants, elephants, elepha

Then he hears someone say they have to shoot the life out of him quick. Or else he will escape this dismal place. They treat him like a game animal at the amusement park. Shoot him for $5 tickets. Why? If we are all made of starlight? He has huge ears. He can taste the world. He can reach out and feel through his long feelers. But he slides and cannot get out of the way of all this.

The writer decides the next time he comes to earth he will be born and he will surely go straight to adulthood. No need for this childhood thing. Forget that. Why would he need such a thing? No need to walk out in the rain. No need to green the grass grows or read the books about Tuffy and Li'l Buddy. Clop clop clop the serious shoes go all the way down the serious staircase.

No! He's gonna walk right out of here! The beasts who take his toys. Now. Let the wolves circle around. Let them circle.

He puts all his notes together. He opens his book and pulls out a pen. The fever is just a gross exaggeration. He doesn't need it. He is shaking. Shakk

To not understand yourself. To float by in this sea of mad-house. To dust off your shoes in the barn and not     see summer     coming    To not     see the leaves     are turning green, the first seeds of spring     To not     see     summer coming?    No!    No!     Don't ever               let this hap-pen.    Don't     ever          let      this        happen.

It has been a long time since the writer has put pen to paper. He will go on. Shaking. Shakk  ing

# SONG

When the belly of the elephant rolls
on top of the strife of this place
then all the stains
will go down to the
towns of this world
roll and roll
all will roll
people will roll
buildings will roll
trees will roll
all across the land
the holy flowers
and the bat men
are so what we have
become
and
the sword is on the ground
and the gristle of war
and the stink is of the pound
and the boat is afloat
and where will we go
where will we go
when we have become one of us
have a good day Mister E.
Step down and lightly
on the dance of bones and whisky
where did you find me
your hands on me
your hands rolling over my chest as you

dawn on me
dawn on me
down down
my head held up high
my great trunk drinking
the twisting as the water cascades
down my egg shaped forehead
earless
you're so close      right next to me
right in me
I am the water
I am the water

I
will be
like water
water.

## ROBERT LOWELL SCREAMING OUT HIS SPEECH IN THE AUDITORIUM AND HE'S TURNING BRIGHT RED AND HIS STOMACH FALLS OUT!

The world has you by the teeth, doesn't it? Admit it, go ahead! The world has you! The world has been stunted by Harvard law school Miggens and Miggens meets Miggens and Miggens and teeth white and frozen smiley smiles! What's all this crap about dry heat? They are frumpy and old and I would rather sit with them than you, Miggins! She has a little quiver to her mouth when she speaks to me. Children are. Children are. I wish I had them. I wish I had been one. Someday I will.

–Robert Lowell

And then I go make a mud pie and play patty cake with the five year old down the street. She has pudgy wet hands that stick to mine as we clap clap clap.

–Robert Lowell (and now his brother Lint is there with him too.)

# DREAMING ELEPHANT WRITES

Plastic Bags
and no teeth
no dentist
the writer says
Our people are a mess!
Cottage cheese skin and
no umbrellas for the people!

# NOTES FOR NEXT PARTS:

1. Robert Lowell is banging on the door to the school let me in he says let me in! I am lonely for everyone! The big men have landed on the rooftop!

2. The students slide down the sides of wet mountains. The first real thing they ever did.

4. At night she crawls back into the air conditioning unit. She has laid it down with old flannel pajamas and a bit of hay.

3. A movie The Writer would like to see made:
   "I need a writer who can write a true story of a man that was a very strong but new Christian, then got mad at God, went out on his own, worked for a bank, stole money to finance drug deals, had all that world could offer, then fell in love again with an old girl friend, they dated, she gave him her purity, bought her wedding dress, then watched as she married another, too much to tell. If you reply, tell why I should let you write my true story. This is my true story."
   —Anonymous

5. I am holding somebody's purse. I don't know whose it is. An alarm clock is going off and a red cat is playing with the Pod People. Someone is murmuring "The Pod People, the Pod People." I must use my imagina

5. He brings her flowers. It is too late. The flowers do not make a difference.

6. I keep dreaming the animals are drowning. Caught in swift currents at sea. Raccoons, opossums, cats and kittens swept and somersaulted into furious currents of oily spills and cardboard boxes and wires and they tumble and you should not want to see the looks in their eyes. Their eyes

do not plead to be saved. Their eyes are not sad or angry. Their eyes shine of sheer survival. Their eyes so wide open it hurts. As the dreamer it hurts so much to look.

6. I am sitting on a toilet in an art gallery and I'm afraid the Pod People can see in.

6. A little donkey is running around on a hillside. I chase after him and adopt him and feed him. He is a very nice donkey and everyone is asking about him and wondering where he came from.

7. He's a small man with large incisors and potato chips stuffed deep into his mouth.

8. Guns. Lots o' guns.

9. And later in the dream it becomes apparent that all the people are pre-programmed to have sex with one another for apparently no good reason.

10. The beginning of one movie is tacked on to the ending of another. The ending of one movie is tacked on to the beginning of another.

11. A movie: A man and a woman are sitting in a restaurant. The man leaves with the woman's scarf. Pretty interesting.

12. *"And suddenly, I looked at the bull. He had this innocence that all animals have in their eyes, and he looked at me with this pleading. It was like a cry for justice, deep down inside of me. I describe it as being like a prayer - because if one confesses, it is hoped, that one is forgiven. I felt like the worst shit on earth."*
   —Antonio Gala

13. Jeanine says, Sometimes I see a light lifting up off of things.

12. *"I saw my city in the Scales, the pans / Of judgment rising and descending. Piles / Of dead leaves char the air— / And I am a red arrow on this graph / Of Revelations."*
   —Lowell

# BUTTERFLY GIRL

The girl stood in front of the jar and it grew wings the color of miracles she stood in front of the jar and it kept growing more and more colors she walked around the jar and came to another jar covered with hundreds of thousands of periwinkle monarch butterflies traveling with huge packs of dogs she told someone about what she had seen and they laughed at her and it hurt that they didn't believe her and then she mentioned volcanoes and a volcano erupted right in front of her just at that moment and then the whole volcano filled up with birds and then the people believed her but then a huge volcano came roaring toward her and roared through her house but everything was fine then she took another walk and she was wearing a flowery red dress and a smaller volcano approached and said do you want a ride she said yes in her flowery dress and so she jumped into the air and the volcano came and caught her and threw her into the air and she spun up in a little twirling dance which felt amazing and then it gently let her down if you know what I mean.

*"Pity the planet, all joy gone
from this sweet volcanic cone;
peace to our children when they fall
in small war on the heels of small
war—until the end of time
to police the earth, a ghost
orbiting forever lost
in our monotonous sublime."*
–Robert Lowell 1967

# ABOUT THE AUTHOR

**Nina Hart** is a writer, performer, and teacher. *Somewhere in a Town you Never Knew Existed Somewhere* is her first book. She lives in Asheville, North Carolina.

www.writingfromthetopofyourhead.com

# ACKNOWLEDGEMENTS

My immense gratitude goes out to the people who helped make the creation of this book possible, including Kevin McIlvoy, Judy Herzl, Philmore J. Hart, Betty Holden, Martha Reich, Gregg Braden, Karuna Haber, Lauren Camp, Teri Wade, Michelle Baker, Kathleen Krupar, Katherine Soniat, Bonnie Freestone, Marilyn Stauter, Josianne Keller, Douglas Gibson, Lindig Harris, and Ty. Thank you for your wisdom, patience, generosity, inspiration, and steadfast encouragement.

Special thanks to all those who so generously donated to my Indiegogo campaign, and to my students, who are a constant source of inspiration. Finally, deep appreciation for my family and my illustrious father Philmore J Hart, a rare human being, who modeled and encouraged the reverence of creativity in me at an early age. In loving memory of my mother, Adelle Hoffman Hart.